Pets Are Awesome!

MY HAMSTER

Norman D. Graubart

PowerKiDS press™

New York

Published in 2014 by The Rosen Publishing Group, Inc.
29 East 21st Street, New York, NY 10010

First Edition

Book Design: Colleen Bialecki
Photo Research: Katie Stryker

Photo Credits: Cover Hintau Aliaksei/Shutterstock.com; p. 5 Michelle D. Milliman/Shutterstock.com; p. 7 Alexruss/Shutterstock.com; p. 9 Pyza/Puchikumo/Flickr/Getty Images; p. 11 Alex Kalashnikov/Shutterstock.com; p. 13 Tom Gowamlock/Shutterstock.com; p. 15 VeryOlive/Shutterstock.com; p. 17 Dmitry Noumov/Shutterstock.com; p. 19 Dragan Todorovic/Flickr/Getty Images; p. 21 Khmel Alena/Shutterstock.com; p. 23 Jane September/Shutterstock.com.

Library of Congress Cataloging-in-Publication Data

Graubart, Norman D.
  My hamster / by Norman D. Graubart. — First edition.
    pages cm. — (Pets are awesome!)
  Includes index.
  ISBN 978-1-4777-2868-0 (library) — ISBN 978-1-4777-2964-9 (pbk.) —
ISBN 978-1-4777-3039-3 (6-pack)
  1. Hamsters as pets—Juvenile literature. I. Title.
  SF459.H3G727 2014
  636.935'6—dc23
                                2013024250

Manufactured in the United States of America

CPSIA Compliance Information: Batch # W14PK3: For Further Information contact Rosen Publishing, New York, New York at 1-800-237-9932

CONTENTS

Hamsters are playful pets.

5

Golden hamsters are the most common pet hamsters in the United States.

Hamsters belong to the **rodent** family.

Pet hamsters live in cages
or aquariums.

You need to feed your hamster every two or three days.

13

Golden hamsters were first discovered in Syria.

Baby hamsters are called **pups**.

16

Hamsters have two stomachs!

Hamsters love to run.

If you take care of your hamster, it will enjoy playing with you.

23

WORDS TO KNOW

golden hamster

pups

rodents

WEBSITES

Due to the changing nature of Internet links, PowerKids Press has developed an online list of websites related to the subject of this book. This site is updated regularly. Please use this link to access the list: www.powerkidslinks.com/paa/hamstr

INDEX

24